AMERICA'S
BLOODY BEGINNINGS

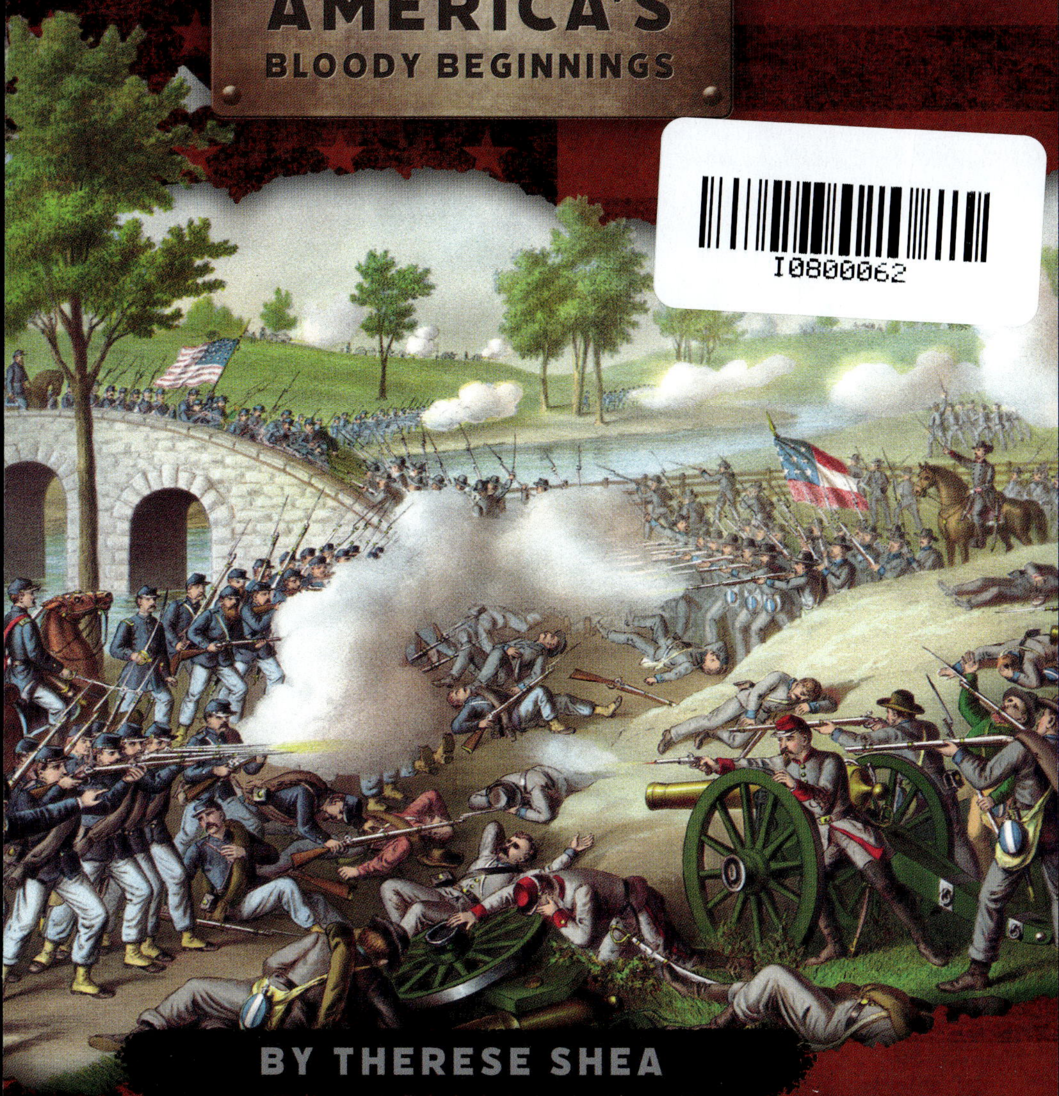

BY THERESE SHEA

THE BATTLE OF ANTIETAM

Gareth Stevens
PUBLISHING

Please visit our website, www.garethstevens.com. For a free color catalog of all our high-quality books, call toll free 1-800-542-2595 or fax 1-877-542-2596.

Library of Congress Cataloging-in-Publication Data
Names: Shea, Therese, author.
Title: The Battle of Antietam / Therese Shea.
Description: Buffalo : Gareth Stevens Publishing, 2026. | Series: America's bloody beginnings | Includes index.
Identifiers: LCCN 2024059393 (print) | LCCN 2024059394 (ebook) | ISBN 9781482472264 (library binding) | ISBN 9781482472257 (paperback) | ISBN 9781482472271 (ebook)
Subjects: LCSH: Antietam, Battle of, Md., 1862–Juvenile literature.
Classification: LCC E474.65 .S543 2026 (print) | LCC E474.65 (ebook) | DDC 973.7/336–dc23/eng/20250203
LC record available at https://lccn.loc.gov/2024059393
LC ebook record available at https://lccn.loc.gov/2024059394

Published in 2026 by
Gareth Stevens Publishing
2544 Clinton Street
Buffalo, NY 14224

Designer: Leslie Taylor
Editor: Therese Shea

Photo credits: Cover (photo) Kurz & Allison, Art Publishers/File:Battle of Antietam2.jpg_commons.wikimedia.org, (series art red texture) Sittipol sukuna/Shutterstock.com, (series art flag) Fedorov Oleksiy/Shutterstock.com; (series art ripped paper) Paul C. Ware/Shutterstock.com; (series art metal plate) Allgusak/Shutterstock.com; (series art caption flag) Rikley Stock/Shutterstock.com; p. 5 Rainer Lesniewski/Shutterstock.com; p. 7 Currier & Ives/File:Bombardment of Fort Sumter.jpg_commons.wikimedia.org, (inset) Everett Collection/Shutterstock.com; p. 9 woodsnorthphoto/Shutterstock.com, (inset) Julian Vannerson/File:Robert Edward Lee.jpg; p. 11 Fasel, A.A., lithographer/File:Battle of South Mountain.png_commons.wikimedia.org; p. 13 Edwin Forbes/File:Edwin Forbes - The Charge across the Burnside Bridge.jpg_commons.wikimedia.org, (inset) Mathew Benjamin Brady/File:George B McClellan - retouched, cropped.jpg_commons.wikimedia.org; p. 15 Library of Congress website/File:Confederate dead gathered for burial at Antietam.jpg_commons.wikimedia.org_commons.wikimedia.org, (inset map) Hal Jespersen/File:Antietam0730.png_commons.wikimedia.org; p. 17 George Sheldon/Shutterstock.com; p. 19 (top) Stephen Kellam/File:Bloodylane.JPG_commons.wikimedia.org, (bottom) Alexander Gardner/File:BloodyLaneAntietam.jpg_commons.wikimedia.org; p. 21 Zeete/File:Burnside's Bridge, Sharpsburg, MD.jpg_commons.wikimedia.org, (inset) Unknown author/File:BurnsideBridge01a.jpg_commons.wikimedia.org; p. 23 Hal Jespersen/File:Antietam1000.png_commons.wikimedia.org, (inset) Mathew Benjamin Brady/File:Ambrose Burnside2.jpg_commons.wikimedia.org; p. 25 Thure de Thulstrup/File:Thure de Thulstrup - Battle of Antietam.jpg_commons.wikimedia.org; p. 27 Charles R. B. Claflin/File:Clara Barton by Charles R. B. Claflin, front- Original.tif_commons.wikimedia.org, (inset logo) Ridex Official/Shutterstock.com; p. 28 Lincoln, Abraham, 1809-1865/File:Emancipation Proclamation WDL2714.jpg_commons.wikimedia.org; p. 29 Alexander Gardner/File:Lincoln and McClellan 1862-10-03.jpg_commons.wikimedia.org.

Printed in the United States of America

CPSIA compliance information: Batch #CS26GS: For further information, contact Gareth Stevens Publishing at 1-800-542-2595.

CONTENTS

Words in the glossary appear in **bold** the first time they are used in the text.

A COUNTRY IN CRISIS

A civil war is a conflict fought within a country and among its citizens. The United States had a civil war between 1861 and 1865. It was the deadliest war the country has ever experienced, with hundreds of thousands of people dying over just four years.

The war didn't break out without warning. The Northern and Southern states had been divided for many years over one issue: slavery. The South relied on enslaved labor for its agricultural economy. The North had developed a manufacturing economy with paid workers. And an increasing number of people, especially in the North and West, saw slavery as a moral issue.

This map shows how divided the nation was in 1861 when the American Civil War began. As the country grew, leaders from both areas had made **compromises** to preserve a balance between states that allowed slavery and those that didn't.

STATE VS. FEDERAL

In general, Southern states wanted rights and powers not defined in the U.S. Constitution to be reserved, or kept, for the states, while Northern states supported the federal government taking more power for itself. For example, the North wanted the federal government to have the power to decide whether new states could have slavery. The South wanted each state to decide.

In 1860, Abraham Lincoln was elected president. Fearing Lincoln's plans for the country, Southern states began to **secede**, beginning with South Carolina in December 1860. Eleven Southern states would secede from the United States in all. They formed a government they called the Confederate States of America.

On April 12, 1861, Confederate soldiers opened fire on Fort Sumter in Charleston, South Carolina. The Confederacy's capturing of this federal property was the beginning of the Civil War. Over four years, fighting took place all over the South, as far west as today's Arizona, and as far north as Gettysburg, Pennsylvania.

Though the American Civil War would be the bloodiest U.S. war, no soldiers lost their lives during the Battle of Fort Sumter, shown here.

Abraham Lincoln

SECESSION AFTER ELECTION

Abraham Lincoln was a member of the Republican Party, which had formed in 1854 to fight slavery's expansion. Before the election of 1860, many Southern leaders stated that if Lincoln won, their states would secede because they believed Lincoln would end slavery altogether. However, though Lincoln was antislavery, he sought to end its expansion at first, not outlaw it.

MARCHING TO MARYLAND

In September 1862, more than a year after shots were fired at Fort Sumter, a battle was fought near Antietam Creek in Maryland. Later called the Battle of Antietam, the conflict had far-reaching **consequences** for the war. It was the deadliest one-day battle in the war and in the entire history of the U.S. military.

The month before, the Confederate army had won the Second Battle of Bull Run in Virginia. This victory and others gave Confederate General Robert E. Lee the confidence to move his army north into the state of Maryland, which was Union territory.

General Robert E. Lee led the Confederacy's Army of Northern Virginia. It numbered 90,000 soldiers at its largest point.

General Robert E. Lee

THE BATTLE OF SHARPSBURG TOO

Some Civil War battles go by more than one name. That's because the federal, or Union, forces often named a battle after nearby natural features, such as rivers and mountains. Confederate forces sometimes named the same battle after nearby towns and buildings. So, the Battle of Antietam was also called the Battle of Sharpsburg, after the nearby town of Sharpsburg, Maryland.

Lee's Confederate army crossed the Potomac River on September 5, 1862, entering Maryland and nearing the U.S. capital, Washington, D.C. They took the town of Frederick on September 7. A Confederate capturing of Washington, D.C., would be a major blow to the United States. Lincoln and the Union forces needed to stop Lee from taking further federal land.

On September 13, Union Major General George McClellan, leader of the Army of the Potomac, received a copy of Lee's military plans, called his Maryland Campaign. Seeing a chance to defeat part of Lee's army near South Mountain, he attacked on September 14. By the day's end, the Union had forced the Confederates there to retreat.

At the time of the Confederate **invasion**, Maryland was a state that allowed slavery. However, Maryland's leaders had decided not to secede.

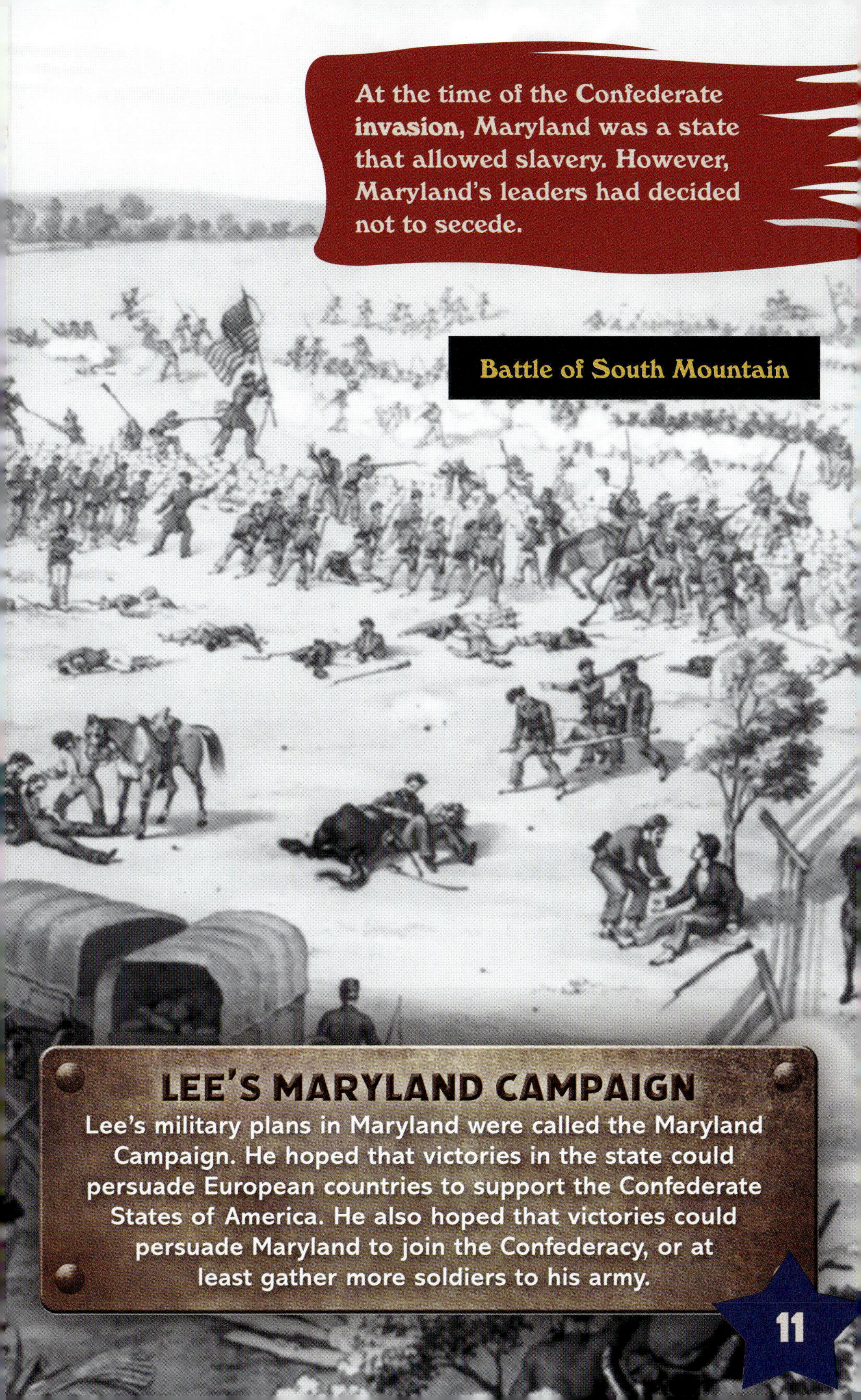

Battle of South Mountain

LEE'S MARYLAND CAMPAIGN

Lee's military plans in Maryland were called the Maryland Campaign. He hoped that victories in the state could persuade European countries to support the Confederate States of America. He also hoped that victories could persuade Maryland to join the Confederacy, or at least gather more soldiers to his army.

CHOOSING THE BATTLEFIELD

Lee commanded his now-divided forces to regroup near Antietam Creek, a mile from Sharpsburg. The area seemed a good one to defend against a Union attack. The creek was deep, and U.S. soldiers would have to cross bridges to meet the Army of Northern Virginia. Lee hoped McClellan's Union army would be easily defeated in the open countryside.

On September 15, Lee's soldiers took positions on one side of Antietam Creek. The next day, they were joined by two more Confederate divisions commanded by General Thomas "Stonewall" Jackson, who were arriving from a victory at Harpers Ferry in West Virginia.

Lee wanted to force the Union army to cross one of three bridges spanning Antietam Creek. These would be three points for his soldiers to target.

Major General George B. McClellan

THE BATTLE OF HARPERS FERRY

The Battle of Harpers Ferry was another piece of Lee's campaign. Fought from September 12 to 15, 1862, "Stonewall" Jackson surrounded and captured a Union **garrison** at great cost to the federal forces. It was the largest surrender during the Civil War, with more than 12,000 Union **casualties**, compared to nearly 300 Confederate casualties.

led by General John Bell Hood. The next morning, McClellan ordered an attack. The Battle of Antietam began at dawn.

Hooker's corps took on the Confederates in a cornfield with help from Major General Joseph Mansfield's Twelfth Corps. This was the costliest part of the day. Hooker lost one-fourth of his soldiers and was himself wounded. Confederate forces were driven back, but Stonewall Jackson's group held its ground at Dunker Church.

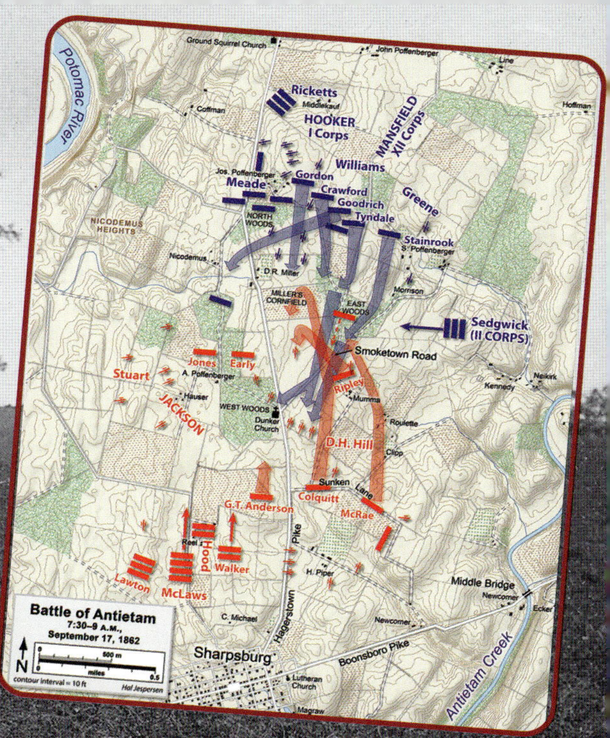

More than 25,000 soldiers fought in and around the cornfield. By about 9:30 a.m. more than 8,000 lay dead or fatally wounded.

A REMEMBRANCE OF BATTLE

The Union lost about 4,000 men in the cornfield. Hooker later described the terrible scene: “Every stalk of corn in the northern and greater part of the field was cut as closely as could have been done with a knife, and the slain [dead] lay in rows precisely [exactly] as they had stood in their ranks a few moments before.”

WEST WOODS

At about 9:30 a.m., Union General Edwin Sumner, leader of the Second Corps, was ordered to back up the Union forces fighting in the field. A division led by General John Sedgwick headed toward an area called the West Woods. At about the same time, Confederate soldiers led by General LaFayette McLaws and Colonel George T. Anderson marched toward the West Woods as well, hoping to help Stonewall Jackson's force.

Soon, fighting broke out between the two sides, with the Confederates having the upper hand with firepower and soldiers. Sedgwick's group lost more than 2,200 men in less than 30 minutes.

The West Woods, a small area of woodland, was the site of intense fighting at Antietam.

RESTORING THE BATTLEFIELD

The sites of the Battle of Antietam are preserved today by the National Park Service. They're working to make the battlefield look as it did in 1862, including planting over 20,000 trees, many in the West Woods. The park service hopes the new trees will help people better understand the history of the area and of the war.

THE BLOODY LANE

The Union divisions under Brigadier General William French and Major General Israel Richardson came up against General D. H. Hill's Confederates in a sunken farm road. Hill's tired troops were no match for the fresh federal forces. They were hugely outnumbered: about 2,200 Confederates to about 10,000 Union troops. Later, another 3,800 Confederates arrived, but too late to hold the road.

After three hours of fighting, about 5,500 troops from both sides lay in the road, later called Bloody Lane. The remaining Confederate soldiers fell back. The Union forces decided not to follow them.

Soldiers also called the sunken lane the "road of death."

McCLELLAN'S MISTAKE?

Union forces had a huge advantage in numbers during the Battle of Antietam, about 87,000 troops to the Confederacy's 45,000. McClellan is often criticized by historians for not using his whole army to defeat the Confederates. He held back after the Bloody Lane fight, for example, when he could have broken the center of Lee's force by continuing the fight with more soldiers.

BURNSIDE'S TURN

In the afternoon of September 17, Union Major General Ambrose Burnside's Ninth Corps finally began its attack. Burnside had received his orders late, and even then, didn't act on them right away. By the time Burnside's soldiers got to Antietam Creek, Lee had pulled most of his troops from that area and sent them to help Stonewall Jackson's force to the north.

Burnside's men were ordered to cross a stone bridge called the Lower Bridge. However, Lee had left about 500 skilled shooters, called sharpshooters, to guard both the bridge and the section of the creek south to the point called Snavely's Ford, believed to be the only other possible crossing point.

Burnside Bridge in 1862

Confederate troops with rifles were stationed on the hill above the bridge. It would take three Union attacks over three hours to get across the Lower Bridge.

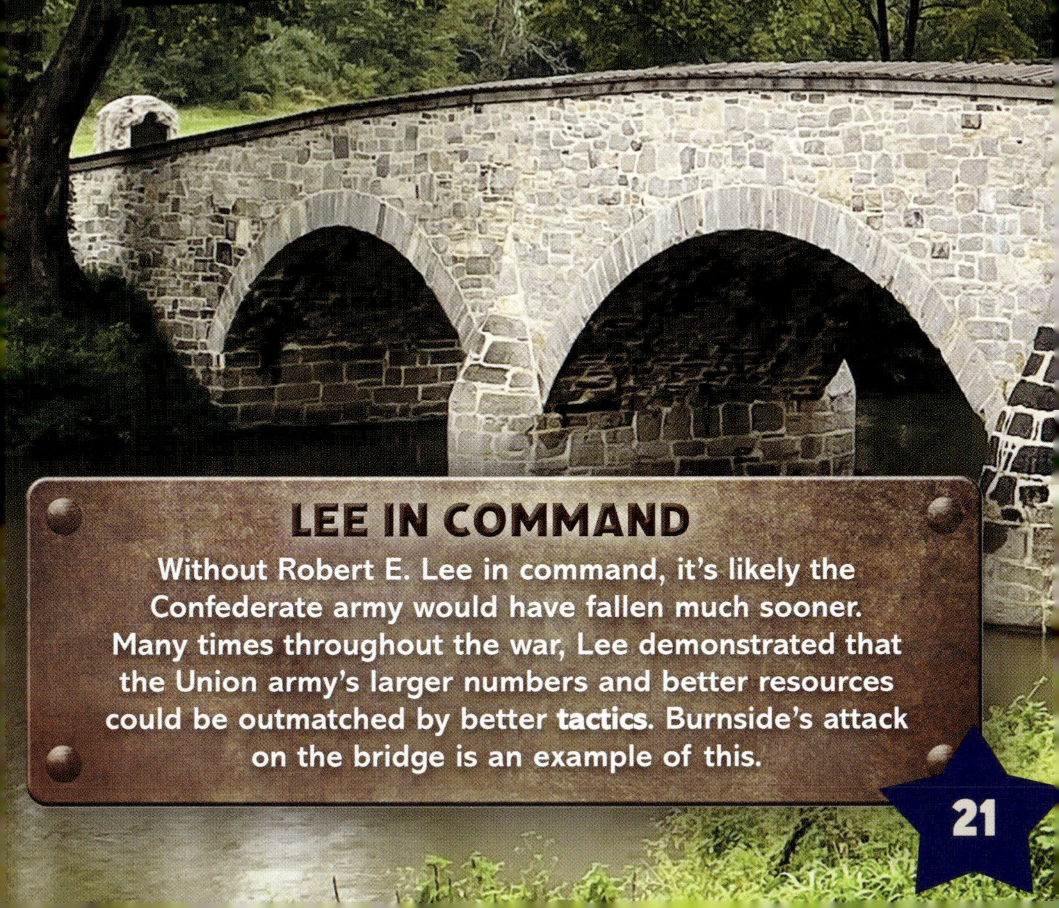

LEE IN COMMAND

Without Robert E. Lee in command, it's likely the Confederate army would have fallen much sooner. Many times throughout the war, Lee demonstrated that the Union army's larger numbers and better resources could be outmatched by better **tactics**. Burnside's attack on the bridge is an example of this.

Burnside's soldiers focused on getting across the bridge. But the Confederates' defensive position around the bridge meant they could easily shoot anyone trying to cross. It was a three-hour nightmare for the Union that only ended when the Confederates had nearly finished with their **ammunition**. By this time, Union troops were charging across with **bayonets**. Another group had successfully gotten across Snavely's Ford. The Confederates were forced to withdraw by about 1 o'clock.

The Union had finally captured the stone bridge, now called Burnside Bridge. But about 500 Union troops were counted as casualties here, compared to about 120 Confederates.

Major General Ambrose Burnside

The events at Burnside Bridge demonstrate how defensive positions can make a difference in battle.

CONFUSION IN THE RANKS

Many criticize Burnside's decision to keep sending troops across the bridge instead of trying to find another place to cross the creek by foot. Some wonder who was really giving the orders. Burnside stated Brigadier General Jacob Cox had "temporary" command of the Ninth Corps at that time. Cox's reports after the Battle of Antietam further reflect some confusion over leadership.

SURPRISE ATTACK

More than 8,000 of Burnside's soldiers streamed over Antietam Creek. At about 3:00 p.m., they attacked a Confederate force of about 2,000. Just when the Confederate defeat seemed certain, another Confederate division, led by Major General A. P. Hill, arrived on the field from Harpers Ferry. The Union troops didn't fire on them at first because Hill's soldiers were wearing Union uniforms. They had taken these from federal supplies at Harpers Ferry.

Hill's troops not only stopped the Union advance but forced them to retreat by about 4:30. This is considered the end of the major fighting on the single bloodiest day in the war.

In the smoke and confusion of battle, the uniform of a soldier is one way to tell an enemy from a friend.

THE BATTLE OF ANTIETAM: WHERE AND WHEN

Cornfield	5:30 a.m.-9:30 a.m.
West Woods	9:30 p.m.-10:30 p.m.
Bloody Lane	9:30 p.m.-1:00 p.m.
Burnside Bridge	9:30 p.m.-1:00 p.m.
Final Attack	3:00 p.m.-4:30 p.m.

These are approximate, or estimated, times that the fighting took place on the battlefield.

LEE WITHDRAWS

General McClellan decided not to pursue Lee's Confederates at the end of the battle. Instead, he expected the battle to continue the next day. That didn't happen. Instead, Lee's troops crossed back over the Potomac River into Virginia, Confederate territory, to recover.

AFTERMATH

The Battle of Antietam is now considered a draw, meaning neither side was the clear victor. However, it ended Lee's Maryland Campaign and drove the Confederates away from Washington, D.C. President Lincoln claimed it as a victory, though costly one.

The South's casualties numbered around 10,315 soldiers and the North's numbered about 12,400. (Casualties for this war included dead, wounded, missing, and captured soldiers.) The exact numbers may be even higher as these numbers are estimates. In addition to thousands of lower ranked soldiers, important leaders, including six generals, were killed on both sides of the field.

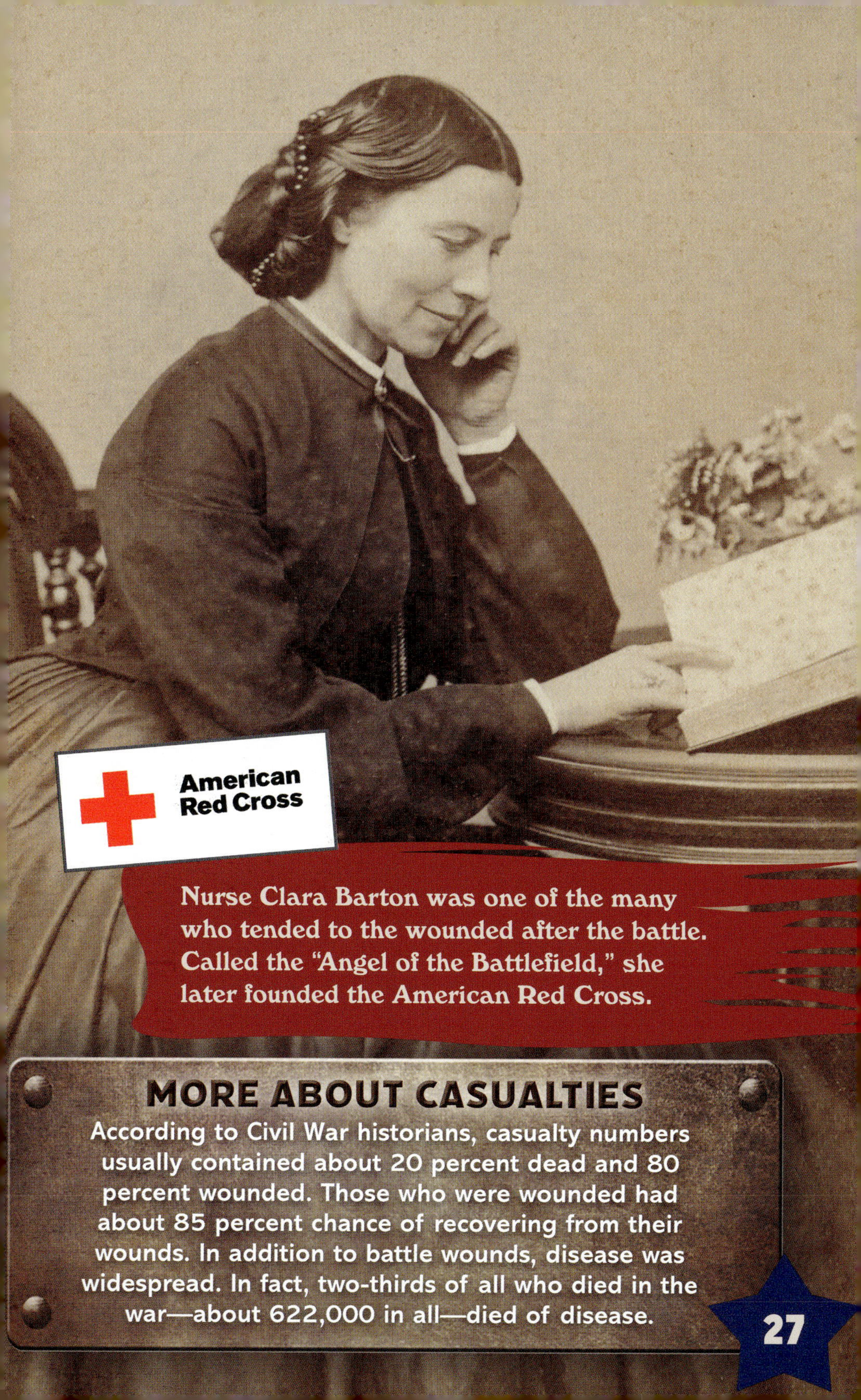

Nurse Clara Barton was one of the many who tended to the wounded after the battle. Called the "Angel of the Battlefield," she later founded the American Red Cross.

MORE ABOUT CASUALTIES

According to Civil War historians, casualty numbers usually contained about 20 percent dead and 80 percent wounded. Those who were wounded had about 85 percent chance of recovering from their wounds. In addition to battle wounds, disease was widespread. In fact, two-thirds of all who died in the war—about 622,000 in all—died of disease.

Days after the Battle of Antietam, on September 22, 1862, Lincoln issued the Emancipation Proclamation. In this statement, he declared that all enslaved people in Confederate-held territory would be freed on January 1, 1863, unless the Confederates ceased fighting. The war became clearly tied to the ending of slavery for the first time.

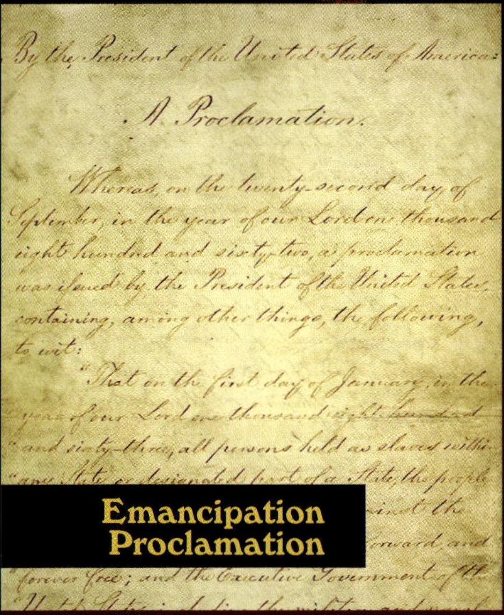

By the President of the United States of America:

A Proclamation.

Whereas, on the twenty-second day of September, in the year of our Lord one thousand eight hundred and sixty-two, a proclamation was issued by the President of the United States, containing, among other things, the following, to wit:

"That on the first day of January, in the year of our Lord one thousand eight hundred "and sixty-three, all persons held as slaves within "any State or designated part of a State, the people ... forward, and "forever free; and the Executive Government of the ...

Emancipation Proclamation

After the battle, European countries, including Great Britain and France, refused to help the pro-slavery Confederacy. Union army **morale**, which had been low after Confederate victories, was greatly boosted. Still, the conflict would continue, with many more bloody battles, until Robert E. Lee surrendered his army to General Ulysses S. Grant at Appomattox Court House in Virginia in April 1865.

Another outcome of the Battle of Antietam was Lincoln (left) removing McClellan (right) as commander of the Army of the Potomac. Lincoln disagreed with McClellan's **cautious** battle plans.

NATIONAL BATTLEFIELD

The area on which the Battle of Antietam was fought became a national military park in 1890. It's now called a national battlefield and contains a national military cemetery and a field hospital museum. The battlefield is open year-round so that people can learn about the battle and its importance in U.S. history.

GLOSSARY

ammunition: Bullets, shells, and other things fired by weapons.

bayonet: A steel blade attached to the end of a long gun.

casualty: Someone who has been hurt, killed, or captured in battle.

cautious: Taking care and paying close attention to avoid risks.

compromise: A way of two sides reaching agreement in which each gives up something to end an argument.

consequence: Something produced by a cause.

corps: A group of soldiers trained for special service.

flank: The right or left of a military formation.

garrison: A military post.

invasion: The entry of an armed force into an area in order to take control of it.

morale: The emotions or outlook a group of people have about tasks.

secede: To leave a country.

tactic: A method for accomplishing a military goal.

FOR MORE INFORMATION

BOOKS

Abnett, Dan, and Larry Hama. *Civil War Battles*. Buffalo, NY: Rosen Publishing, 2024.

Lyons, Brendan J. *Charley: The True Story of the Youngest Soldier to Die in the American Civil War*. Havertown, PA: Brookline Books, 2023.

Silva, Sadie. *The Civil War*. Buffalo, NY: Enslow Publishing, 2023.

WEBSITES

American Civil War
kids.britannica.com/kids/article/American-Civil-War/352967
Learn about the rest of the war.

Antietam National Battlefield, Maryland
www.nps.gov/anti/index.htm
See what the battlefield looks like today.

Antietam/Sharpsburg
www.battlefields.org/learn/civil-war/battles/antietam#
This site includes an animated battle map.

INDEX